Breaking Waves

by Hope Moore

Printed in the United States of America.
First Printing, 2022
ISBN 9798847111041

www.Byhopemoore.com

Cover Image: Kenneth Carpina
Cover Design: Hope Moore

BY HOPE MOORE
Let's heal together

"After all, computers crash, people die, relationships fall apart. The best we can do is breathe and reboot."

-Carrie Bradshaw, *Sex and the city.*

Dedication

I dedicate this book to everyone who has been heartbroken.

Table of contents:

Remember, there is *beauty* in the *breaking.*

Collapsing Waves

<u>Overflow</u>

I used to have cravings,
For the way you made my heart beat.
It used to push through my ribs.
It would ruthlessly crush my lungs,
And you were the only thing,
That could swoop in to revive me.
It's still like that now.
It fills the air differently though.
My heart is still managing to beat,
But the raw pain is unbearable.
You aren't here to ease it.
You are the cause and the cure.
If there's an antidote,
I don't know where to look.
All I can feel is this pushing,
This plunging, pounding,
A raging wave of emotions,
That only has plans to overflow.

Demise

I tried to swim in the deep parts of his heart.
Unaware of the gallons of oil within.
Thick and life-threatening as it filled my lungs.
The drowning didn't bother me,
I was happy he finally let me in.
Even if I met my demise from inside.

Tornado

Our love was a destructive tornado.
Chaos was our silent partner.
Always latched onto our backs.
As we annihilated each other.
And every time I spread your soul,
Shattering it across the debris.
I only wanted to renovate our home.
Just one more chaotic time.

Fragmented Letter

As I search for the words to connect into fragments.
That I cannot speak without burning my tongue.
I find the indescribable expressions of truth,
Written in ink, laid out open and bare.
Burn this letter once you've read it.
I'm not sure you deserve to linger or feel,
These broken sentiments I've left here for you.
To re-read these woes and shattered dreams.
Your language isn't fit for this memory,
But your hands have held hotter things.
Like foul wordplay from your mouth.
When you yearned to feel superior to me.
So let this letter quickly burn in your palm.
Vanishing into ashes, the only remnant left of me.

Burned

I burned the pages of our love story.
As the smoke traveled into the sunset.
You were nothing but a pile of ash now.
I released your dusty remains into the sea.
Hoping the wind and tide would take you.
To a coast across the world, away from me.

Feel

I wanted to incinerate my emotions.
To destroy the lingering and aching pain.
That established a home within my heart.
Releasing the voices inside my mind,
As their hollow waves screamed for me to *feel.*
And I couldn't outrun the weight of the vibration.
The despair pursued me quicker each second.
Nothing would silence the screech of my emptiness.
With each twist and jerk on every concealed door.
I discovered there was no way to escape,
The core trembling emotions, demanding to be *felt.*

The Others

Love can be daunting.
After encountering people like you,
How will I break down my walls?
I did that with you.
I kicked down my walls for you.
With no hesitation, I was finally ready.
But when you betrayed me,
The bricks moved in unison.
As they formed thicker walls.
They evolved taller now too.
They tower over hundreds of cities,
To look out for people like you.
I cringe at the idea of a new lover,
Because my mind constantly screams,
"Please don't be like the others."
And I hate that I dare to compare,
You to someone else despite the despair.

Bitter

You were like gas station coffee.
An aging pot with a bitter batch.
As much as I hated the foul taste,
That no sugar or cream could erase.
I needed you to start my days.
To stay awake and feel useful,
In the middle of your draining world.

Cherry Vines

Your words are like cherry-soaked vines.
That tightly wrap around my tongue.
Slowly inching closer in each minute.
As they compel me to yearn to speak,
And eager to stay quiet, speechless.
To devour your tale, whether truth or lies.
As your sweet flavors seep into my body.
Stealing every voice of reason within me.

Laced

Your words were laced with poison.
So every time I let you bite me,
I slipped further into the darkness.
You consumed me in your web.
And I surrendered with no hesitation.

Tricks

I dipped my finger into the pond.
I gazed into the shimmering reflection.
And I watched as my touch made ripples.
That gracefully splashed against the ducks.
I saw your face over my shoulder.
Only to swiftly turn around to nothing.
I was yearning for another beautiful sight.
Often, my eyes play tricks on my mind.

Twisted Hope

You are my anxiety.
You trickle down my skin,
Like sweat from a hot flash.
I feel your presence nearby.
It crawls over my chest.
Like a microscopic spider,
That has a taste for flesh.
So, I know you'll be back.
You'll sneak back into my life.
Through the tiny cracks,
That multiply all over my heart.
Just to leave open possibilities.
To have some sort of twisted hope,
That you'll feel the cold draft.
As it whistles for you from the inside.
And maybe you'll be the warmth,
That I always needed.
But you are just a panic attack,
You are my anxiety.
You trickle down my skin.
I'll keep repeating these words.
Until this love for you,
Stops feeling like a sin.

Web

The web of your deception captures me.
A tenacious trap that never allows me to be free.
Unless I bow to you, willingly on my knees.
Vowing to be by your side and never flee.
But can't you hear my chains? They're all I see.
As they scrap like blade-filled waves beneath me.
My shrill screams echo within this dark-deep sea.
Do you tune out my voice and let things be?

Rip Tide

We got caught in the rip tide.
We were swept out to sea,
Lost amongst our chaos.
We never found our way,
Back to shore, back to love.

Warning

There was a silent warning.
Hidden within the fierce wind.
It screamed for me to get out.
To be free of my steel chains.
A tropical storm was on its way.
Making its course through your body.
As it pleaded its case to leave your mouth.
To drown me in your raindrops of sorrow.
Clogging and infecting my eardrums.
So I couldn't hear the ways to escape.
Submerging my threatening brown eyes,
Until my vision was clouded and blind.
Searching frantically in the dark,
For my safe haven during the flood.

A Case

You were just a mystery.
I have always been a detective.
So, my mind couldn't resist,
The task of figuring you out.
I was inclined to pursue you.
You weren't the first fugitive,
That I chased from border to border.
Because at the end of the day,
What is a detective without a case?

Moss

I clung to you for life,
For entirely too long.
I was a tiny but budding tree.
I hoped you'd water my roots.
But you drowned me instead.
Moss grows over me now.
It's taken permanent residence,
Upon the tip of my bark.

Exile

It feels like my brain is an enemy.
An intruder to my fragile soul.
The way it vibrates unwanted energy.
It travels directly into my heart.
It releases memories of you,
And I want nothing more,
Than to send it into exile.

My Call

Do you hear it?
This faint heartbeat reaching for you?
As I gaze into the crescent moon,
The same one you're admiring.
Like we used to on Autumn nights.
Hoping you'll feel my energy, *my call.*
From your cracked window,
Miles across this echoing city.

War

The war is raging.
This relentless battle,
Between you and me.
I'll consider a truce.
I'll wave this white flag,
If it means I'm free of you.

Sinister

Your love feels sinister.
You are the spider crawling down my back.
The creaking floorboards in my room.
My bathroom light that flickers at two am.
You're a dark entity lurking in my halls.
You creep into every single room,
You manipulate every inch of my space,
And you love watching the haunting of me.

Reparations

I want my reparations.
For the damages caused,
To my breaking heart.
That's the least you can do.
After stripping me of my home,
My love, my soul, and my friend.
I'm talking about you.
But in an unfortunate way,
It resonates with me too.
You left with me in your hand,
I guess you took both of us.

Realities

I watched you shove,
A dagger into my heart.
You didn't blink, not once.
As my last tears dropped,
Following my lifeless body.
Staggering over me at your feet.
I tilted my head up to look at you.
I begged for mercy from the pain.
And you just walked away.
Yes, it was a nightmare, a dream.
But someone whispered to me,
"Dreams are alternate realities."
If that magic is fact,
It seems you break my heart,
In every single universe.

Tastelessly

You are injustice in human form.
Your infidelities went unnoticed.
They lingered under the surface.
Hiding in between your lips,
Within each kiss we shared.
It's funny how you cheated,
And somehow, she left no taste,
Upon your used lips.
You cheat tastelessly.

Turbulence

I told you that my heart was fragile.
Every time you carried me away,
You moved with turbulence.
Like an airplane in a violent storm.
With no regard to the way I may break.

Flight

On that gloomy day, you fled the city.
You left me a card and a dozen roses.
They sat, abandoned on our coffee table.
Here were your last words, placed with such grace.
But laced with a wreaking stench of a runaway.
As if this four-dollar card with cheap words,
And fading red roses from the corner store,
Could amount to what you could never say.
You are an elegant failure of flight,
Tainted with a cowardly soul.

Fool

I've been searching for the right words.
The perfect choice of selected letters.
That could somehow describe it all.
Only I was a fool to think I could.
You, us, what we were, it's indescribable.

Weapon

I isolated myself,
Confined to the walls,
Of my overactive brain.
Days soared like hours,
As I tortured myself,
Every single second.
You were the weapon.
A blade dipped in us.
You know how toxic,
Your love is to me.

Doom

The sunset of doom.
It marks another day gone.
Another day stuck in your gloom.
Another night I'll be up until dawn,
Stuck in a self-constructed tomb.
Unaware that I'm so withdrawn.
This heartache is all I consume.

The Untouchable

The paranoia climbed my spine.
I was afraid of the untouchable.
No one would believe my screams.
That vibrated across cities.
At the grimmest time of each night.
You were coming for me.
To annihilate me once again.
Maybe it was only nightmares.
And every morning when I would wake.
I would feel you over my bed.
Drilled tightly into my head.
You are the untouchable my love.
Too fast to outrun within my mind.
You're a drug too addictive to unlove.
But I'm tired of being confined.

Wilt

After the thunderstorm of you,
I wilt like an over-watered rose.
It's funny how you once helped me grow.
Only to destroy everything I've become.

Daydream

I'm stuck in a sad love song.
It kills me to sing along.
But what else can I do?
This ongoing loop of you,
It consumes my mind.
Happiness is hard to find.
All I can do is daydream,
Of a time when singing,
Didn't turn into screams.
This love song is stinging.
Like bees around sunbeams.

Broken Words

Your broken words cascaded upon me.
Like a random and severe rainstorm.
They cut inches deep into my heart.
Now I'm stuck lost in a dictionary.
One full of the wrong words,
And no clue to which ones,
Hold the key to repairing my heart.

Wrong Places

What if I'm my own ghost?
The eerie bump in the night that I fear.
The entity inflicting my own haunting.
Maybe I've been searching for monsters,
In all the wrong places.

Stubborn

You were so selfish.
Like a three-year-old,
Who doesn't love the concept,
Of sharing their favorite toys.
I would blame your parents,
But I'm sure they tried.
See, you are stubborn.
Like a coffee stain,
Fighting the detergent,
For a spot on my white shirt.

For However Long

I taste you in my salty tears.
As I lay down to rest, into a dreamless night.
Praying to yearn for you no longer.
This unattainable desire for your scent,
Lingers throughout the hallways of my mind.
A fragile scrapbook made of feelings,
That I can't seem to stop reliving.
How shall I go on? I have no idea.
Within these bittersweet memories of you,
A broken soul is weeping within me.
Waiting for the pain to cease, to vanish into the air.
But I haven't gathered the strength to tear the pages.
My deepest intentions are to stay wrapped in you.
For however long I can, however long it lasts.

Victim

I hope you follow me home.
I've left tire tracks for you.
Down that long and dusty road,
That leads straight to my driveway.
Just to make it a little easier for you.
As you find your way to me again.
How delusional have I become?
To lead the vicious killer,
Straight to its helpless victim.

Shelter

Our love caused tidal waves.
They'd rip through the sea,
As every creature within,
Scurried to find shelter,
From the forceful impact.

Almost

I see your face in old polaroid's.
Faint images you took of me.
Late nights on our rooftop.
I hear your voice in my vinyl.
As the record player plays,
Your favorite nostalgic records.
I feel your fingers tracing mine.
And it almost *feels real.*

Before

Dismembered dreams,
Lost amongst the broken.
I want to pull them,
Down from the clouds.
To put the pieces back together.
Just so we can remember.
The type of love we envisioned,
Before the beginning of the end.

Without Me

I want to wish you well.
Send you off into the sun,
Tell you to *"be happy."*
But I can't find the strength,
To mutter those distant words.
I'm more than selfish, it runs laps,
Through my blood and I'm honest.
I don't wish to see you happy,
Especially when it's without me.

Plague

You are a deadly plague.
You creep into my lungs.
You steal my last breath.
Weaken my body and soul,
And you watch as I gasp for air.

Incision

This thick slice in my heart,
It will always be reserved for you.
You made this irritated incision.
How can you not watch me bleed?

Mend

I am a dumping ground for broken souls.
I attempt to mend them, and I always fail.

Invitation

I'm a hopeless romantic.
Naturally, I accepted.
That cordial invitation,
To fall in love with you.
I should have declined.

Repressed

Your heart was a home,
For repressed trauma and rage.
It expanded and left no space.
It was no surprise to realize,
You couldn't love me properly.
Even if you attempted to try.

Caution

You walked into my heart,
Wearing flashing caution tape.
You were dripping in yellow.
My mind manipulated my eyes.
I saw a massive pink ribbon.
Perfectly placed on an angel.
I was blind to the warning.

<u>Crumbled</u>

You rolled over my beating heart.
Like an eighteen-wheeler over concrete.
And just the same, I crumbled under pressure.
I disappeared into rubble that only kept breaking.

Eyes

My eyes always told the truth.
They'd cry streams of blue tears.
Every time you left the house,
And I had no idea where to.
They'd scream in agony.
Every time you'd ignore me,
Instead of hearing my worries.
They lost more of their dazzle.
Each day I looked into your eyes.
Only to see another woman,
Staring back at me through them.

Blame

This love,
It will shred us to atoms.
It will tear us down to limbs.
It will rip our hearts.
It will incinerate our minds.
It will leave us shattered.
It will take and destroy,
And there is no one to blame.
Except for one another.

Nightmare

If I allow you to sneak into my dreams,
Will I be able to keep you forever?
Is my mind the one place you feel safe?
Because every time I'm awake,
You are a recurring nightmare.

I Hope

I hope you cry bloody streams of tears.
That may sound too dark, and it feels harsh.
But I hope you can't sleep every single night.
I hope you are tired, fighting a hundred demons,
That look just like you, so you know how it feels.
I hope peace never finds its way to you,
And restlessness follows your every move.
You can write me off as bitter or cold.
I do not mind, and since that is so,
Allow me to crawl into your mind.
I hope to be your biggest haunting,
I will devour your heart in every nightmare.
I wish to see your soul turn into stone.

Until

That sparkle in your eyes faded.
It used to twinkle in rainbow hues,
Every single time you looked at me.
Like I was the only girl for you,
Until I *wasn't.*

Still

After all this time has escaped us,
The sun still rises to greet the moon.
The lakes still swirl to meet the oceans.
And I still love you like you're still here.

Elusive

Your energy was so ill-lit and elusive.
And I've always fallen fondly on mysteries.

Hostage

There were times I wished I would fight.
Hold your heart hostage and make us right.
Let you in, again, just to let you hold me tight.
Then maybe I'd forget the pain for a night.

Art

I will engrave you into my heart.
I will weave you into my soul.
You will be embedded into my poetry.
As you will forever be my muse,
Of heartbroken forms of art.

Fed

He unleashed his desires.
I was not enough,
For the appetite of a monster.
He *needed* more,
He desired to devour *more*.
He's well-fed now.

Poison and Antidote

Your eyes held secrets only I knew.
Like the reasons I loved you unconditionally.
They told the tale of me, captivated by you.
Embracing everything perfect and flawed.
Falling deeper into the depths of your eyes.
Oh my, the way they would make love to my soul.
But your eyes possessed secrets that only I knew.
So you were able to carve out all my best qualities.
Trapping me in a web weaved by your hands.
Luring me in, seduced by our intoxicating love.
I was stuck in a sticky trap without wanting to be set free.
Yearning for one last drop of us to roll down my tongue.
Traveling at high speeds until it crashed into my heart.
Although you were poison to me, I begged for more.
Just another day, a month, or a year, twisted in our love.
Your eyes were my poison and my antidote.
Both killed and revived me.
With each slow gaze into my eyes.

Illusion

Your love was an illusion.
It was never really there.
But it looked like love,
It smelled like love,
It felt like love.

Stars

On starless nights,
I gaze into the sky.
Looking for something,
Anything that can suffice.
I cautiously dip my hands,
Into my changing imagination.
I manipulate the indigo sky.
I fill it with illuminating sorrow.
Because without the stars,
What will lead you home?

Shame

I should've known it wasn't going to end alright.
A bomb tick-ticking, with neither one of us to blame.
Tears swallowed our love through each night.
As we drifted further into our bed of shame.

Erupt

I have a massive volcano,
Living within the walls of my heart.
I feel as though at any moment,
I'll erupt spewing scorching lava.
Only to serve as a needed release,
Or a symbol of this pent-up anger.
That has been boiling in my chest,
Ever since you betrayed me.

Roses

Scattered rose petals.
Withering away under my feet.
A used symbol of love,
Now completely unrecognizable.
I stomped and skinned them,
Of any remaining hues of beauty.
The fingerprints tainted on the thorns.
The off-guard and elusive act of love.
That you desperately attempted and failed.
What good can these roses serve?
They only showed up at my door,
To ease the gnawing guilt eating at you.

Poetry

I've always written poetry.
So, transforming you into haikus,
Has never been a struggle for me.
But with you, my pen craves more.
It craves detailed memoirs,
Suspenseful romance novels,
Horror films that are way too long,
And catchy heartbreak songs.
With you, poetry isn't enough.

Gallop

You needed to heal.
So instead of taking your hiatus,
You decided to use me.
I was the horse to bear your trauma.
As you would ride me,
Until my feet grew weak.
You never once stopped,
To ask if I was okay.
You were on a journey to healing,
By the power of me.
I guess I could've stopped you.
Standing tall on my feet,
And refusing to gallop.
But I've always had a soft spot,
For those in need.

Hurry

There's a room in my heart,
With your name engraved on the door.
I keep the sheets tidy, and the pillows fluffed.
I dust your bookcase and antique paintings.
I open every book you love to your favorite page.
Then I hope it tempts you to hurry home.
But I know you won't.

Us

I took pieces of us in my suitcase.
The day I left, and you let me.
Our love is fleeting, broken...
So, I allow my mind to dream,
Of distant fragmented memories.
No, not of the days we argued too loud.
But the days we laughed so hard,
The entire building heard the echoes.
The nights you'd stay up writing songs.
Only to sing them to me in the morning.
These fragmented memories.
They trick me into believing we were okay.

Passion

We had so much passion.
It drove us to insanity.
I never thought it would.
They told us we need passion.
It's the only way to know love is true.
But passion is a: 'Strong and barely,
Controllable emotion.'

5:08 am

5:08 am nightmares of you.
They creep under my door,
To infiltrate my mind with pain.
You haunt me every night,
And you don't get tired of doing so.
You show up at the same time,
Ready to bring me a taste of hell.

Bite

You thrive in chaos, terror, and fear.
You were always a rabid animal.
I should have sent you off with a label.
But I'll write this poem instead.
I hope she's reading this right now,
The next girl in line to get bit by you.
I promise you she'll call animal control.
Your bite, your heart, it is frightening.
I hope you see my face,
When they stick that needle into you,
And you fade away, as *she puts you down.*

Stability

I craved stability for so long.
I started to scramble the meaning.
Like eggs but burnt to a crisp.
Sporadically, as I tend to do.
Mistreatment by the same heart,
That was my idea of being stable.
I rather fight the monster I'm used to.

Haunted

I'm stuck frantically searching.
I've rummaged through my heart.
To find happiness or peacefulness.
I feel haunted in the simplest term.
Not haunted like a ghost is in my house.
I'm haunted by the memory of our love.

Flaws

The list of your flaws,
It's more than extensive.
Like Marvel film credits,
It seems to never end.
Except with you,
There's no sneak peek.
No extra must-see scene.
It's just you and your flaws.

Glue

You were my biggest disappointment.
Out of all the hearts I've healed,
To see yours collapse once again,
In a repeated relapse for the last time.
I couldn't bear the core trembling pain.
Of seeing you shattered and scattered,
Across our living room floor.
I knew I didn't have the strength,
To glue you back together *again.*

Sunrise

Your ghostly memory,
It dangles from my ceiling.
As I lay in bed, tucked in tight,
Staring into the abyss of you.
Hours start to feel like days,
And I can't wait till sunrise.

At Battle

I'm so angry at you,
While in rage with myself.
I allowed this to unravel,
Right before the eyes of my heart.
I felt that something was coming.
I shut every set of blinds,
I tuned out the noise of the world,
And I pretended everything was fine.
I can be upset with you.
But I'm at battle with my mind.

Parasitic

You are more than draining.
That would be an understatement.
You suck life with just a touch.
You look into souls and destroy them.
Your only goal is to score, to leave the game,
Holding the most hearts, the most pain.
You are the worst kind of parasitic leech.
You drain and drain, you never get enough,
And how could you ever fill that void?
That excruciating hole that keeps growing,
Becoming darker, deeper, and more daunting.
In the exact spot where your heart should be.

Pen

I write with a pen full of heartbreak.
I reach out for better words,
Words that smell like sunshine,
But the only words to leak from my pen,
Smell like they've been laced in storms,
And tainted by enormous dark clouds.

By Fire

I sentence you to death by fire.
So you can feel your heart burn.
In a never-ending pain, like mine,
On the day you set us to flames.
And watched our love burn,
Into black ash right in your palm.

Survival

I wake up just to live another day.
To have another coffee,
To watch another show,
To find another job,
To buy another purse,
To do this, to do that, to do anything.
Anything other than think of you.
Anything other than think of life,
This mess, this fight, this war,
That I may or may not win.
But I'll have another strong coffee.
I'll watch ten more great shows.
I'll find a few more tolerable jobs.
I'll buy way too many purses.
And maybe then you and this life,
Will be nothing but another dream.

Dusk and Dawn

At dusk, I feel you inching nearby.
By dawn, you've consumed me.
As if my terror is routine for you.
All the hours in between,
Are filled with my aching cries.
I'll try to outrun the thought of you.
And maybe next time I'll succeed.

Seesaw

When you're on a high,
It seems like I'm on a low.
Why can't we feel good together?
I thought we were parts of a whole.
As we play on this seesaw of love,
The cycle is never-ending.
You go up, and I go down.

Worth

You snatched my happiness,
Like a thief after rare jewels.
I guess I should be happy.
That it was worth so much to you.

Three Hundred Meters

I was soaking in pain.
My heart felt like it was beneath water.
Crushing under the intense pressure,
As we floated deeper into the abyss.
How is it I see your face?
When I'm three hundred meters down,
Pushed to my ruin by your hand.

Possession

Your possession gripped me tighter,
With each "you can't wear that,"
That fled through your lips.
My acceptance of you grew closer.
With each "okay" that I muttered.

Airbag

Your love crashed into me like an airbag.
Quickly pushing to protect my heart.
Only you were the car that caused the collision.
You left out that part.

Candlelight

You became darker,
As I became lighter.
I thought you'd follow,
Soaking up all my energy.
So we could both shine,
But you didn't.
You fell deeper into the dark.
No matter how many times,
I set fire to my wick,
You blew out my candlelight.

Cartoons

You fumed colossal puffs of red.
Like the men in old cartoons,
When they used to get angry.
The smoke pushed through their ears.
As if a chimney lived in their head.
You'd release your anger like that.
I wish I could draw you differently.

Missed

You dismissed all my calls.
They all went missed.
Every *"call me back,"*
I cried on your voicemail.
Only to be left unheard.
Any chance at closure,
Gone, the call…
Never returned.

The Mud

I've never been one to,
Run to my friends.
Or even social media.
After a breakup,
I used to unplug,
And turn inward into me.
Internalize my pain and work it out.
But with you, everything is different.
I feel a heavy and steady long pull,
To drag your name through the mud.
Until no one even recognizes you.

Shards

You broke me,
Into thousands of tiny shards of glass.
When it was time to gather the remains,
Not only did the remnants of me,
Slice the tips of all my fingers.
I couldn't muster up one idea,
On how to make myself whole again.

Consumed

The anger consumed us.
As we inhaled its toxicity,
And exhaled its violence.
It infiltrated our bodies,
And we allowed it to happen.

Water

You were toxic to me,
As I needed you to breathe.
Like water, capable of drowning me.
Dragging me thousands of feet under.
Flooding my lungs until I stop fighting.
But before it submerged my entire body.
It was required to keep my heart beating.
To supply me with hydration and energy.
You are like miles of ocean leading nowhere.
As you forced me to need you every day.
While you knew you could launch me,
Into the harsh wilderness of your control.
Watching me sink into a dark-freezing pit.
With an anchor tied to the front of my lips.

Dysfunction, Malfunction

Wrapped in dysfunction,
You arrived at my doorstep.
Like a Christmas gift under the tree.
The one I wasn't expecting,
But it's there, tied with a purple bow.
So, I'm thankful, and I unwrap it.
Only to find that you tend to malfunction,
And you were final sale with no returns.

Days Ago

Life moves quicker than planes in the sky.
Just a few days ago, we were together.
We sat at the Starbucks and shared a loaf.
We laughed about our day at work,
As we planned our summer vacation.
Today you're thousands of miles away,
We haven't talked in about five days,
And the memories of us are fleeting.

Insecurities

You lured out every one of my insecurities.
That had been hibernating for so long.
You reminded them why they exist.
The moment you cheated on me with a girl,
Who had everything that I wanted to be.

Key

If communication is key,
Locked doors surround us.
We are left alone with no combinations,
No resources or a way to *escape each other.*

Urgency

By any means necessary?
I guess, when it comes to yourself.
Because when it trickles down to me,
There is no urgency, no necessity.
I am a post-it note filled with chores.
Taped onto your rusty fridge door,
Aging faster than every milk carton,
That sits rotting inside of its walls.

Mosquito

You sucked all my love,
Like it was blood you craved,
And you were a starving mosquito.
That I should have swatted away.

Rooted

I'm tired of being like this.
I wake up with the sun,
Breathe, and start the day.
I stay up with the moon,
Thinking of you.
The clock keeps flipping,
My heart stays planted,
In the deep-rooted soil,
Of everything, we used to be.

Empty

I never liked being alone.
Especially on cold nights,
When my house is empty.
The air lingers differently,
And all I desire is a feeling.
The feeling of your body,
Wrapping around mine.
You *were* the best warmth.

Burnt

Disgusted by you,
By your memory, our love.
I want to incinerate it all.
I want to leave nothing,
But ashes and burnt hopes.

Lust

Can this lustful behavior,
Ever evolve to taste like love?
Can you give me something *like love?*
You carry mountains of baggage,
Heavy tons, all *dripping in lust.*

Things I Wish I Knew:

1. Our love will rip me apart.
2. I'll lose myself with you.
3. Your temper will boil over.
4. You'll cheat a few times.
5. I'll cheat back a few more.
6. I'll hate your inconsideration.
7. You'll think I care too much.
8. We will destroy each other.
9. Our love will be addictive.
10. We'll miss the chaos.

Risky Tendencies

I've always had a love for risky tendencies.
So, when they warned me about you,
I still chose to pursue your love.
Little did I know, you were the riskiest,
Out of all tendencies I've indulged in.

Rescue

You could only give me false hopes.
Next time, I won't be the savior,
The one that throws you the rope.
To rescue you from your behavior.

Motives

Only if I knew your motives beforehand.
Maybe that's my fault, I should have asked.
But maybe, just maybe, it's yours.
You were the one wearing a hundred masks.
Orchestrating a thousand games and plays.
You are an Academy award-winning actor.
Take a bow, can we have an encore?
You are the master at deceiving.
You manipulated your words,
Only to hide your true motives.
Now I sit here, with a mind full of regret,
And one question stuck on a loop,
Was it all really *my fault?*

Giver vs Taker

You were a taker.
I was a giver.
We fed off each other,
We fueled the addiction.
The more I gave you,
The more you wanted to take.
And as you took more,
I only replenished the supply.

Ring

Fire is everywhere.
It surrounds us.
It circles like a ring.
One step out,
I get burned.
I guess you lit the match,
In the perfect way.
To ensure I'll stay trapped.

Unrequited Love

I never thought that you'd be my unrequited love.
I never even thought I would have this *kind* of love.
See, growing up as a girl like me, I believed in fairytales.
Yes, the kind of fairytales like Cinderella and Snow White.
I thought love would show up on my doorstep,
At the perfect moment in the most perfect way.
I never heard of the princes who don't return love.
The kind who would never settle down with a princess.
They left out that part and painted love in the best image.
And unfortunately, I haven't had that yet.

Cain

They called him a Cain.
I'm not religious but,
He shined like Abel to me.
Unknown energy,
That I craved to pursue.
So, I fell in love with him.
And I wish I hadn't.

Master

You are a master at playing with emotions.
And I am the master of playing along.
We are the worst kind of combination.
We only fuel the fire of our destruction.

Corrupted Love

You poisoned me with your heartless lies and deceptions. You were like a black hole, dragging me down with its suction. Days, and nights, alike, you'd explode like volcanic eruptions. Trying to keep me tied to you, with tales of aged sex and seduction. Plotting on my soul and sanity waiting to act on your abduction. You lured me into your pitiful life cluttered with corruption.

Oil and Water

Our love clashed in the heat.
We mixed like oil and water.
We reached our boiling point.
It was too late to fix us.
Our anger popped and burned,
The surface of our hearts,
Every time we tried to mend things.

Fight

It was never going to end alright.
At times I wish I put up a fight.
Combated your ego and made us right.
Let you in and allowed you to hold me tight.
Then maybe I'd be able to sleep at night.

Brick By Brick

I tried building us a happy home.
You'd forcefully knock it down.
Aiming to wreck it brick by brick.
Hoping to bury me in the rubble of us.
Leaving me stone-cold and heartbroken.
In a hole rooted so deep in the ground,
Underneath your feet as you'd roam around.
Abandoning me in this dark abandoned ditch.
And you keep coming back to push me down.
As I frantically try to stay alive inside,
To find my way out of the debris-filled hole.
Crying to the universe for the strength to get out.

Better

They say I'm better off without you.
All you did was cause me pain.
So why is my heart still bleeding blue?
The urge to see you is hard to maintain.

Platter

You mocked my love.
You sliced open my heart,
Placed it on a gold platter,
And fed us to the world.

Cat and Mouse

Maybe you cursed me.
This scent of dread,
Resentment and rage.
It follows me,
I try to hide and outrun it.
But every time I do,
It lurks and searches for me.
As a cat hunts its prey.
And just like a mouse,
I get caught every single time.

Love (Acrostic)

Linger within my heart,

Open and free to roam.

Valiant and determined.

Eager to explore my realms.

<u>Hate (Acrostic)</u>

Having been here too long,

Anger consumes your being.

This heart you have inhabited,

Extracts *"too much"* of a heavy toll.

The Loss

I've been mourning the loss.
The out of sight, out of mind.
The puppy that has been lost.
The heart left stranded.
The roaming mind in the clouds.
Me. I am the puppy, the heart,
The mind, I am lost, I am the loss.

Envy

Let's talk about the envy you bleed.
The viscous sticky substance in your veins.
It seeps into your skin, feasting on you.
As it oozes green slime from your lips.
Each time your mouth is fixed to speak.
To only scream of your intense need.
Of the things, you don't have.

Pull and Take

This cycle is repetitive.
We are stuck in a toxic cycle.
We pull love, and we take the hate,
Until there's nothing left to seize.
The last one holding the most,
Well, they *win.*

Torment

If some higher power is out there,
And it meant to cause us no pain,
Why did it create souls like yours?
It feels as though you were crafted.
Made perfectly for my torment.

Intruder

I was living in a walking casket.
I was alive but dead at the same time.
My body felt like a stranger,
My mind felt like an intruder,
And my heart felt like it wasn't mine.

Fairytales and Fables

When you told me your zodiac sign,
Why didn't you tell me you were emotionally abusive?
When you told me your favorite movie,
Why didn't you tell me you were insecure to the core?
When you told me your go-to comfort food,
Why didn't you tell me you had volcanic-type anger?
When you told me you wanted to love me,
Why didn't you tell me you desired to destroy me too?
You sold me fairytales and fables.

Break

We were so in love,
We made cupid jealous.
Somehow, we grew thorns.
Our words became harsher,
Our hearts drifted further,
And our minds needed a break.

<u>**Gaslighting**</u>

You called my concerns childish.
You blamed me and my feminine.
I'm thinking too much.
I'm being too emotional.
You were the king of gaslighting.
My mind was your throne.

Still

I write until my fingers wither away.
And still, the pain you left is here.
I sing until my throat breaks,
And still, your memory is on a loop.
I paint until I can no longer see darkness.
And still, your face is burned into my mind.
I attempt to cut these ties and heal from you,
But still, I'm stuck in the cycle of heartbreak.

History

History repeats with us.
We love,
We argue,
We betray,
We hurt,
We leave,
We miss,
We come back.
I hope to rewrite history.
My wish is for the end.

Abrasive Nature

Your abrasive nature flourished.
You were demanding and blunt.
Picking my flaws like apples,
During Autumn in apple orchids.
You took a bite of my insecurities.
Hoping to digest and transform them,
Into something favored in your liking.

Ninety-Five

Only if I chose door number ninety-five,
Behind that door, a five-star vacation waits.
Behind the other is a one-way ticket home.
Like those old game shows.
I went for door number eighty-two,
And I ended up with you.

Trigger

Inside the barrel of your gun,
My love for you sits dormant.
Hiding within a deadly bullet.
Waiting for you to pull the trigger.
As this undying love for you,
Will soon be the end of me.

Depression

Sometimes I feel like a basket case.
Constantly crumbling like concrete,
Into piles of depression and memories.
And it doesn't yearn to stop.
It shatters and quickly multiples,
Into towers of rubble stacked to the sky.

Shed

Some demons,
Intimately sway with the angels.
They allow their souls to reshape,
And transform with every stride.
Seducing one another,
To surrender peacefully.
To humbly submit to love or pain,
And shed away their ways.

Someday

It's cold and weird here now.
In this bed where we slept for years.
So much love shared within these walls.
They echo in waves of heartbreak now.
I refuse to listen, I will sleep in peace,
Well, *someday.*

Dread

There is no hopeful tomorrow.
You took all the hope I had left.
Now, when the moon is awake,
I see the unpredictable future,
Dressed from head to toe in dread.

Timeline

I wish I could press rewind.
On the remote control of life.
So I can go back to the moment,
I gave you my phone number.
And rewrite the timeline of us.

Lie

You lie like its air.
As if you need it,
To simply breathe.
But no, you need it,
To keep control.
You buried the truth.
So I'd stay with you.
Lying is your control.
Why lose me?
When you're a lie away,
From paradise.

Accepted

I accepted you.
I took in your venom,
I hoped it wouldn't kill me.
No one ever fathomed that.
They never understood why.
Now, I don't think I do either.

Delusion

I've seen hell,
Or some version of it.
I would say, "baby, you're not it."
But that would be a mouth drowning,
In delusional insanity-filled lies.
You just might be the closest thing,
To an actual walking hell on earth.

Closed

You turned off your ears,
When I needed to speak.
The words begged to flee,
Soaring faster than a bird,
As they pushed at my mouth.
I was yearning for a response,
That could answer all my doubts.
But you kept them closed,
With your mouth sealed shut.
I guess you'll never know,
The steps that could've saved us.

Numb

Laying under the glowing moonlight, I ponder.
How have I gotten as hopeless as they come?
My mind roaming lost, like a butterfly off to wander.
The more I lose my mind, the memories become fonder.
Pain fades like dust into the air as I begin to feel numb.

Gone

Irritation slept in our bed.
Cuddling the sore parts of us,
Each night we drifted to sleep.
So many cold winter nights,
Both of our hearts freezing over.
And we didn't want the warmth,
We could get from each other.
How couldn't we see,
That our love was already gone?

<u>United</u>

My mind exploded into darkness.
Once I slipped into a night of dreams.
Where I found you, just a suit and bones.
Standing alone on the polished ballroom floor.
I whispered my final goodbye into your ear.
And even your ghost stole my heart too.
As your icy breath sent chilling waves,
Down my spine, my core, and into my heart.

Parts

I have written you a hundred letters.
I sent them off with the doves,
Into the grey sky dripping in sorrow.
I signed them with the ink of my heart.
Sincerely, the remains of my broken parts.

Soon

I've been mourning you.
Like you've passed on.
Only you are four miles away,
Our hearts are untouchable.
But I still talk to the moon,
I play my guitar under the stars,
I dance in fields of wildflowers,
And I hope I forget you soon.

Puzzle

I can't accept that we aren't meant to be.
Every time I try to, my heart aches.
I remember the way our souls loved.
During heavy rainstorms at night.
Our bodies fit perfectly together.
The missing piece to my puzzle.
Now, I feel I'll never be complete.

Dawn

Between dawn and the gutting of my heart,
I see you mocking my pain over and over.
With your hand inches into my chest,
Ready to take everything I have left.
I wither away within the moment,
My strength fades, and I set myself free.

Burn

We moved too fast.
We didn't learn enough.
We didn't laugh enough.
We didn't love enough.
In some other universe,
I hope we go slower.
We understand each other.
We enjoy one another.
We showcase our love.
We have a slow love,
One that takes its time to burn.

The Shore

Starved Heart

I consumed days waiting near my phone.
I watched as every piece of me drifted.
Each fleeting further away like trailing dust.
That the harsh wind quickly swept away.
Your withered ways became old to me.
In between your weekly distant calls,
Dreary days of your missing person games,
And hideous lies rooted so deep like weeds,
That could never get pulled out.
The excitement to still hear your voice.
To know you were in some way *there,*
No longer satisfied my starved heart.

Rabid

I ran out of love for you.
Or maybe I just ran out of excuses.
I lost the ways to explain your behavior.
The ability to transform you was fleeting.
I could no longer bear the heavy weight,
Of turning a rabid monster into a prince.

Ending

I wanted you to destroy mountains for us.
To fight every battle that stood in our way.
But you didn't have the strength or the will.
So, with my heart bruised and abused.
I boarded the first plane leaving the city.
Headfirst into an unknown and new chapter.
As soon as we reached the sky, I closed our book.
I vowed to stop re-reading the same old story,
While hoping for a different ending.

Spiraling

As my heart fell from ninety stories high,
Uncontrollably spiraling to the pavement.
I fearfully whispered my breathless goodbye.
With my helpless body paralyzed on the roof.
I stretched my mind to the stars in the sky.
Begging for a sign or guide to find love again.

Puppet

I'm happy he's gone.
I was dependent on him.
It took almost losing myself,
To see that I was already lost.
I was already breathing,
By his hand, like a puppet.
Every move I made,
I thought it was out of love.
But it was blind control.
He'd always hover nearby.
Infiltrating my thoughts,
And directing my actions.
Now he's gone,
The strings have been cut,
I have no puppet master.

Lingered

The hate for you lingered.
It overwhelmed my soul,
And it snatched every piece,
Of love I had for you left.

Remnants

My pen has forcibly entered a drought.
This seeping ink will not surface for you.
My worn pages no longer have the room.
For me to fill with piteous thoughts of you.
You carelessly steal every single inch from me.
Leaving me with nothing but my cold mind.
So I burn the branding you've placed upon me.
There's nowhere to free your charred remnants.

Property

I'm free to love myself now.
You stole every ounce of me.
I lost my love for my laugh,
My waist, my curls, and taste.
I will retrieve every piece of me,
That I allowed you to seize,
I want my property back.

Manipulation

If I had loved you any longer,
I wouldn't have seen the red flags.
As you were concealed in my words.
Every time I spoke of love,
I thought you were speaking of it too.
I didn't know that our love was conditional.
Only existing by the strength of my blindness.
And the inability to see you for what you were.
As I was doused and marinated in manipulation.

Won

I refuse to return to you.
This heart won't relapse.
I won't surrender my peace,
To a battle, I already fought.
To a war, I already won.

Piece

You climbed forbidden mountaintops.
While searching through forgotten forests.
To recover the pieces of your shattered heart.
So you could retrieve every single shard.
As you were attempting to mend your soul,
To tend to your brand-new open wounds.
After he made the incision and left in a hurry.
Like a speedy wind during a long harsh hour.
He had to outrun the explosion of your emotions.
Dodging every lost piece of you that headed his way.

Disaster

What a beautiful disaster it is,
To fall blindly in love.
To bear the weight of heartbreak.
And bloom like a rose,
When you were once withering.

Myself

I used to mend souls,
While never protecting my own.
I never thought that my helpful nature,
Would be the cause of my demise.
So, I stopped transforming hearts.
I stopped mending bruised souls.
I took all that misused love,
And I poured it back into myself.

Nirvana

I've finally reached nirvana.
I've transcended into abundance.
I am overflowing with happiness.
I am finally breathing freely,
Of your consuming toxicity.

Stolen

She speaks, and you hear melodies.
They pulse and flow from her mouth.
As they flood your bruised eardrums.
They submerge your damaged heart.
And swallow your injured ego.
Only to leave behind peace and flowers,
That multiplies and consumes you whole.
She helped you bloom, and what is left?
You leave behind dead leaves and decay.
You engulf everything beautiful about her.
You destroy and chop up the melody,
And you take the pieces you need.
But she is ever flowing with rhythm.
She holds the pitch in the pit of her soul.
You think you've stolen it all,
While you've already been caught.

Dreams

All you offered me were dreams.
I needed to touch the stars.
I needed to reach the clouds.
I needed to shatter the sky,
Intertwining with the sunsets,
With no plans to come back down.

The Bees

Some days, the bees sting my heart.
On others, they feed on my sweet nectar.
They pollinate my blooming soul.
They stockpile it in honeycombs.
Until I slowly drip thick honey.
That sweetens the bitterest teas.
And heals the sore throats of the sick.
The bees may hurt,
But they have a purpose.

Destiny

You jilted me at the shore.
Now that you're gone,
The sun shines brighter.
The sand feels softer.
The waves plunge greater.
I drink the sunshine,
And devour the moonlight.
I thought I was stranded,
But I found beauty in the stars.
I found a friend in the trees,
Love in the seas, weeds, and bees.
Your departure was destiny.

Cages

You had this lock on me.
But I found the key.
I no longer find comfort,
Within the bars of cages.

Healing

The darkness screeches so loud.
When I steer into the abyss of my mind.
Lush green forests overwhelm my thoughts.
The thick branches swallow every star.
I fall stranded amid unfamiliar territory.
Moondust dances off my nose from the sky.
Guiding my eyes down a luminous stone trail.
That I follow through the silence of the night.
By the time the sunrise greets my eyes,
I'll escape the lifeless dark one last time.
With a feeling of healing weighing so immensely.
I'll hold my mind beneath the rays of the sun.
And I'll allow the raindrops to submerge my heart.
As Daffodils takeover and bloom through my soul.

Alone

I realized that I deserved to be respected.
Such a small thing that should be natural.
You lacked it all together.
So, I found respect for myself.
It was like a miracle right at the end,
Of a movie that lasted way too long.
Then I left you in that hallway.
Exactly where I found you,
Alone.

Power

I am the one that got away.
You will search for my love,
In everyone after me.
And that is the best power.

To Feel

Some days, I feel alive.
Like I can climb any mountain,
To the center of its peak.
I feel fierce and unstoppable.
On other days, I feel depleted,
I lack ounces of energy and drive.
Then, I realize life isn't a constant high.
The lows will wash to the shore of my life.
But only to show me how great it feels,
To be destroyed.
To be empowered.
To feel *everything.*

Our Song

For the first time since the end of us,
Memories whistled from my radio.
As our song started to play.
And for the first time, they didn't win.

Free

My shackles echoed as they hit the ground.
I dug myself out of your pit of a heart.
I fought to strike the surface of sanity.
I was finally free of the trauma and you.
The sun hit my skin, and I glistened.
The air attacked my lungs, and I laughed.
My heart was a feather, serenely floating.
My soul began to feel replenished.
I was ready to live without your limits.
On those cold nights, you wanted to break me.
But you were the curse bound to be broken.
And I'm simply brimming with happiness.

Blissfully

At a point, I felt blissfully lost.
I was discovering myself again.
With every wrong left turn,
Each step still felt right.
Wherever I was going,
It wasn't back into your life.

The Storm

The storm is a part of the journey.
The rain must fall, it must be.
All beautiful things may drown.
Until the sun uncovers her eyes,
And sends massive waves of blooming.
Into every living thing in need,
Like Lilacs, Pumpkin Ash trees,
And the sore hearts of you and me.

Over

The heartache is over.
The season of pain has passed,
I'm free to love, to feel, to be happy.
I'm blooming differently now.

Saved

I slowly became empowered.
By him and the heartache.
I dug myself out of the ruins.
I took control of my fate.
My power saved me.
Self-love saved me.
Wisdom saved me.
Without the heartache,
Where would I be?

Hope

I found comfort in pain.
I was stuck in the storm,
Drowning my soil,
Preventing my growth.
Until I found happiness,
And fell in love with *hope.*

Ecstasy Bolts

Lightning bolts full of ecstasy,
Strike the ground beneath my feet.
Blasting them throughout my body.
Releasing their power to every piece of me.
I float upon the clouds of happiness.
This infectious energy won't allow me to fall.
So, I'll just rule this beautiful storm.
Making the sky my throne, castle, and all.
Striking the hearts of the lost and sad souls.
That needs a dose of ecstasy to take control.

Sympathy

My sympathy ran dry.
I tried to feel sorry for you.
Like you were somehow a victim.
Of societal pressures placed on men.
But this city nor your weak friends,
Forced you into a bed that wasn't mine.

Dies Out

I reflect on our tornado love.
I remember how it swept me up.
Like paper tossed in circles,
By strong harsh winds.
I feel the pain for the moment.
Then it slowly dies out like a flame.
I am a force too strong for that tornado.
I never thought this could happen.

Heal

I feel the need to heal greatly.
It crashes against my heart,
Like high tides colliding into rocks.
I spill out my deepest emotions.
And I release them into the sea.

Bled

Toxic love fled my heart,
As I bled out every drop of you.
I screamed in a consuming rage,
But also, in a happy awakening.
I finally chose myself,
Finally.

Dear You

The sun runs laps in your mind.
Don't spend a second in worry,
About the storms that may head your way.
Has anyone told you that you shine?
You soak up every puddle of water,
Only to release each drop into the desert.
To bring relief to the ground in a drought.
You are every miracle fulfilled,
Just by breathing right now, at this moment.
So, stay strong because *you are strong.*

Release

Rest, feel, and release it all.
The thoughts, the memories, the pain.
Write it out, cry it out, scream it out.
Find your healthy habit and heal.

Melody

I was left breaking and lifeless.
My heart barely made a beat.
Between each faint pound,
I thought *this* could be my end.
But how foolish would I be?
To allow you to steal my melody.

Honor

She is naturally vivacious.
Her smile is alluring.
Her eyes are arresting.
Her heart is limitless.
Her mind is intriguing.
Her soul is incandescent.
To love *her* is an honor.

Dice

The moral of the story is,
You misused me.
You toyed with my love,
You played games.
You used my heart as a set of dice,
As you tossed it across the floor.
So, I used yours as a deck of cards.
I began to dance in your mind,
And I took control of the game.

Intrusive

I let go of my intrusive thoughts.
They riddled and rippled with pain.
They'd tie my brain into knots,
Securely bolted with steel chains.

First Song

When the birds sing their first song,
I'll finally let go of you for today.
Healing is a lingering process.
Some days I feel lost without you.
On others, I feel found all alone.
When the birds sing their first song.
I know that I will be okay.
I'll sing along to their tune,
No matter my mood.
Healing is an ever-evolving process.

Harbored

I put the feelings I harbored for you in storage.
I could no longer bear to witness their decay.
As feet of dust collected upon their surface.
Time snatched pieces of me every day.
To add to the box filled with your remains.
I was still here, and life didn't stop at passing.
My wings had yet to take flight into the sky.
So I packed you away, but the pain still stayed.
But maybe I lived for me that day.

Discarded

We? No, *me.*
You lost the right to that word.
The day you discarded us.
Like a used greasy napkin,
That no longer served a purpose.

Vanished

When the last leaf fell from the tree,
I knew I had to let go of you.
When the sunset vanished,
And the moon was the only light left.
I had to find my way home by myself.

You Are More

There have been so many men that called you pretty.
Before they acknowledged your strength and ambition.
As if all you had to offer was a beautiful face.
They overlooked your intellect and kindness.
To quickly glance their eyes upon your thighs,
Counting the inches between your skirt and your knees.
Like you were made to be walking eye candy for them,
Or a supermodel, waiting to be signed and critiqued.

Meal

As if this half-empty mentality,
Could ever serve me for long.
I have a hunger for healing,
And I must have a meal.

Serenity

After spending so long within dark walls,
She finally got her dance with the light.
The radiant sun soaked into her cheeks.
Her smile was ever-growing.
Stretching from New York to London.
With lingering notes of serenity and love.

Battle Scars

It seems that with every colossal heartache,
We are left with thick battle scars.
Embrace them and their markings.
Because they are a beautiful symbol.
They are the forces of your past.
Resting upon your skin,
To show you how strong you are.

The Names

If these battle scars had names,
They'd be called Betrayed,
Misused, Regret, and Lost.
But these scars hold no power.
So, I renamed them Happy, Alive,
Growth, and Healing.

Color Blind

Do not feel worthless,
Like your art doesn't shimmer in value.
Some may not see the hues of you.
The reflections of crimson and scarlet,
That dance upon your beautiful face.
Your worth is not appraised,
By souls who are color blind.

You Will

I promise that you will heal,
From all the pain you endured.
The weeping-filled nights alone.
The feelings of worthlessness.
The burning rage that heartbreak left.
You will heal.

Aligned

I chased my feelings away.
They occupied too much space,
Within the tiny rooms of my heart.
I bottled them into airtight jars.
I hid them deep within my mind.
I depleted them of their forceful energy.
I gradually allowed them to die.
But I should have set them free,
To flee into the burnt orange skies.
As I'd move on to brighter places.
And they'd weave into me peacefully.
My heart, soul, and mind,
Perfectly aligned.

How To:

I could write hundreds of poems about you.
This never-ending heartache you've inflicted.
But I'll write thousands of books instead.
How to: heal from the clutch of a broken touch.

I Laugh

I look back now, and I laugh.
At you? Oh, absolutely!
But I also laugh at myself.
My vulnerability,
My hopefulness,
My stupidity.
Every time I saw red flags,
And swore they were blue.
Every time you showed me,
Love didn't live for me in you.
And I thought I could conjure,
Some little feeling out of you.
I look back, and I laugh.
I remember how silly you are,
Then I move on.

A Petal

Flowers bloom here now,
The first petals reach the surface.
They fly through the realms of growth.
Leaking love from their stems.
With each one I pick,
I'm a petal closer to healing.

Only Choice

You deserve to be his only choice.
In this life and your next one.
Even if you come back as a golden eagle.
Lost amongst rainstorms and magenta skies.
He should find you without clues or a plane.
When your weak wings give up.
The moment they can't endure another flight.
He should carry you through a million cities.
To get you home, every single time.

Bell Chime

No growth nor elevation,
You loathe in inconsideration.
I quickly lost my patience.
I can't keep you down.
Every time I attempt to,
I throw you right back up.
You are a toxin to my body.
An intruder loose inside my mind.
You are a waste of my time,
I'm losing the magic of my prime,
I'm letting you go once the bell chimes.

Journey

Sometimes healing feels like you're still bruised.
Like the wound is closing but is tender to the touch.
Be patient with yourself on the journey.

Earthquake of Love

Our love was built on a fault line.
So the bricks would shake often.
They would crumble under the intensity.
Of every forceful rattle beneath our feet.
Burying us within the rubble remnants.
Just so we could claw our way out.
To rebuild our love into a home, again.
Using the same worn pebble-sized brick,
That cracked under immense pressure.
With nothing binding it but cheap super glue.
A cycle that is consistently repeated on a loop.
After each devastating earthquake to our love.
We fed the cycle of rebuilding once more.
When we should have just moved.

Scoop

Keep scooping your happiness,
Like your favorite ice cream.
Scoop until you hit the bottom,
Leave nothing but milk and sugar,
Dripping from around the rims.
Feed your soul the taste of peace.

Phases

Caterpillar, cocoon, butterfly.
Evolution, the smell of growth.
Some days I feel stuck in place.
The caterpillar phase lingers,
Then suddenly, it's over.
But now, the cocoon won't break.
I'm still without my wings.
And the final version of me,
Still feels stranded galaxies away.
Healing is slow, growth is slow,
Every phase will wither to an end.
So, I'm patient, *it's coming.*

Gold and Brass

I found my worth, finally.
Not within you, how presumptuous.
Within myself, and that's how it should be.
A soul like yours could never appraise me.
I was searching for my gold-like energy,
While stuck inside your sea of brass.

Honey

Your love hurt,
Like a sting from a bee.
So, I wasn't surprised,
When thick honey,
Began to seep from me.
Thank you.

Moving On

Maybe they had a reason.
To crush your soul,
Leaving you dripping in blue.
Completely drained out of love.
But that doesn't matter now.
You're moving on.

Life

Sometimes it will feel like,
The world makes less sense now.
Like once the love faded,
And the relationship ceased,
Your life seemed to follow.
But how could that ever happen?
It *followed* them as an illusion.
It hid in the shadows behind you.
How can you appreciate life?
If you don't know how it feels,
To think it has all slipped away.

For Fun

You turned me into this savage.
How are you confused?
When I tear your mind apart,
And step on your heart for fun?

Venom

You bit into my foolish heart.
Spewing a vicious venom.
That uncontrollably leaked,
Into every ragged pocket of my existence.
Poisoning everything, I used to love.
As you were careless, you didn't think.
That it would include all my feelings for *you.*

Far Away

My worth no longer lives in you.
You were only a temporary home.
I've moved to a sunnier city,
Away in mind, far away from you.

Muse

She is the epitome of a muse.
Her eyes swirl into the paint,
That you use on your canvas.
Her soul lingers in the lyrics,
Of every love song you write.
She is exploited in every scene,
That you direct in romance films,
That are marinated in her heart,
And ever dripping with her mind.
I would say she lives within your art,
But she controls your craft.
She is your art.

<u>Ash</u>

If I'm not good enough for you,
I'm not sure who can be.
As I've tried to make miracles,
Out of nothing but dust and ash.
Just to make you see me,
As *"worthy"* of you.

Rain

Heartbreak reminds me of rain.
The downpour inconveniences us.
But there's a higher purpose.
The roses will bloom.
The grass will grow.
And just like heartbreak,
The rain is a miracle,
That only leads to healing.

Gratitude

Give yourself daily gratitude.
Appreciate yourself more.
You are the hero of your story.
Act like it.

Heartbreaks Bloom

Every painful heartbreak blooms.
It evolves into self-care and healing.
The clouds may be dark right now.
The storm may take a while to end.
But you will grow from it all.

Healing Stuff

I got a missed call.
The ring echoed,
Through my mind.
I felt it was her.
The anticipation,
As I grabbed my phone.
It chilled my spine.
It was her, she called.
After months spent,
In a deafening silence.
She finally called.
I'd been waiting for that.
And when it got there.
I didn't even call back.
That's the funny thing,
About this healing stuff.
It's unpredictable.

Opposites

We were like,
Fire and ice.
More than opposites.
Stubborn and unwilling,
To learn from one another.

Icicles

This frozen heart of mine.
It's cold to a touch of love.
I don't know when,
These icicles will melt.
I don't know who,
Is warm enough to melt them.
So, I'll start defrosting it,
With the strength of my love.

Oasis

I found an oasis of love,
Amidst the growing hate,
That filled my lungs.
I held my head high,
I embraced the light air,
And the wind of my finesse.

Perfectly

After we broke up,
I started to notice the world.
Like that old brick road.
The one near downtown.
We walked down it every day,
But I never even noticed it.
It has some of the oldest shops,
The most stunning churches,
And extraordinary, beautiful souls.
The sun shines on the block perfectly.
And I think it does so purposely now.

Grow

The storm clouds will break.
The light will crack through.
The rain will soon cease.
The wildflowers will grow,
And so will you.

Desert

I felt like I was stuck in a desert.
With no sight of water for miles,
And no will left to keep fighting.
I was so stuck, dwelling in the end.
That I didn't see the escape hatch.
It rested right underneath my feet.
Only after tumbling down,
Did I find there was an ocean.
Plunging and waiting for me.
The whole time.

Soil

I bloomed into power.
It danced on my petals.
It strengthened my thorns.
It drenched my thick soil,
To gracefully transform me.
Into the powerful woman,
That you stole away from me.

Crown

I replaced my crown of pain,
With a stronger gold one.
Made from the fire of my soul.
Made with power and happiness.
A queen should never wear,
A crown decorated in sorrow.

Robbery

I used to let my lovers consume me.
I thought that was true love.
Giving every ounce of my being,
To the person, that I'm in love with.
It was standard nature for me.
I wasn't coerced into a confession.
And they aren't completely innocent.
But I must acknowledge my wrongs.
I aided and abetted my own robbery.
As I gave them so much of myself,
How can I say they stole it all?

Half-lit

I let go of the regrets.
The *what ifs.*
I was not the cause,
Of his deceitful nature.
I pulled stars from the sky,
To light up his dull life.
And he still searched,
For a *half-lit* fleeting flame.

Refueling

I exhausted my energy.
Wasted on failed efforts,
To revive our memory.
I'm refueling now,
It's time to fill my spirit.

<u>Never Think</u>

My emotions are raw.
Fresh and delicate.
They sit here arranged.
Into words and pages.
I hope you never *think,*
That my art is for you.
You are a damaged,
And toxic kind of muse.
What kind of poet would I be?
If I didn't turn you into poetry.

Talk

A four-letter word,
It means so much.
Talk. Talk. Talk.
I only wanted you,
To express yourself.
In a better way than,
Unpleasant faces,
And distant energy.
But your lips always,
Stayed sealed shut.
You pushed me out,
And I finally gave up.

Pathetic

I rose from the ashes of you.
I flatlined and revived myself.
Just to laugh at your face.
As I arrived on your doorstep,
To mock your massive failure.
A pathetic homicide attempt.

Equation

I found the strength,
To pull my heart out.
I'm subtracting myself,
From the equation of us.

Ghost

Meet me in the middle.
On a cobblestone pathway.
So I can confront the ghost of you.
After the raging storm of pain passes.
When I can see you through the mist,
As the trail of your darkness follows.
Let me invite you to hear my tale.
Of the days spent in turmoil with you.
Before you escaped into a shadow.
Refusing to acknowledge your emptiness.
And the way you attempted to drain me.
Once I'm done, I'll leave you under the trees.
The ones that harbor decaying leaves.

Forgive

I chose to forgive him.
The scars may never clear.
But the wound will close.
My heart had to release,
My mind was forced to let go,
If I wanted to heal properly.

Element

The fierceness in my voice returned.
The power in my walk grew stronger.
The vulnerability in my heart felt safe.
I shined brighter and I healed quicker,
I've never felt more in my element.

One

The moon greets the sun.
As the light retreats into darkness.
Swirling lakes intertwine with seas.
It reminds me of myself.
The way I weaved into one,
With my heartbreak, naturally.
I transformed it into healing.

Things

I started to do my favorite things.
Like watching romance movies,
Drinking tons of cappuccinos,
And devouring novel after novel.
I lost touch with the little things.
The small pleasures that ease me.
I'm taking care of my soul now.

Unchained

I undressed my heart.
I made love to my mind.
I caressed my soul.
I became my best lover.
I unchained myself.
I fled that confining castle,
I bloomed into my savior.
When did I ever need a prince?

In the End

When I was younger,
I thought romance movies were dramatic.
A guy who could never seem to settle down,
And the girl who is left crying and somehow,
Picked by someone and finds love in the end.
It's funny how it always ends like that.
Either a reconciliation with the inconsistent lover,
Or a new prospect who treats her perfectly.
Why is it never the girl loving herself in the end?

Need

I poured so much love into you.
I'm taking it all back.
I'm drenching myself in love.
I need it now.

Pinky Promises

During spring in kindergarten. The scent of bubblegum was in the air. Pink chalk scraping the sidewalk. Hula Hoops whistling in motion. Me and my best friend. Sitting on the creaking bench, Pinkies interlocked and cramped. As we promised to stay friends forever. And we did. I thought about that moment. The day you stood before me and broke every promise you made. See, I find that traditional gestures, ancient myths, and superstitions; may unfold to be true. That would explain why your promises, held no truth nor did they bear any weight. Unless you pinky promised too.

Balance

I won't forget the good moments.
They still ring in importance.
I must embrace the balance.
The good and the bad.
The lost and the found.
Everything has a purpose.

Escape

Good girls wait for love.
We're told to sit, legs crossed,
And stay pristine for our prince.
But what happens to the good girl?
As the prince acts like a peasant?
With no signs of nobility or royalty?
We escape the castle.

Deep-rooted

Some days heartache lives in my bones.
On other days happiness lives in my heart.
Often, deep-rooted regret lives in my soul.
Most days, healing lives in the soil.
The only way my spirit grows every day.
Heartbreaks will wither away,
But healing will always stay.

Route

I was trying to love myself.
But I had a few steps wrong.
I tried to validate myself,
With how he felt about me.
I got lost on the route to self-love.
And that was my first mistake.

Versions

I am art,
Formed from a genocide,
Of hundreds of thousands,
Different versions of me.

Red Ink

I'll cross out your name.
From my heart, my mind,
My poems and my songs.
In red ink, so it feels real.
I'll erase the traces of you,
That leave behind footprints.
Upon every blank canvas,
That I never get to use.
I'll use them now.

Pit

I set healthy boundaries now.
Step too far over this line,
And you must go.
You will fall into my abyss.
We no longer cross boundaries.
I'll push you into the pit,
And allow you to drown,
In the mud of your disrespect.

Watered

I check in with myself now.
I make sure my feelings are watered.
I assure my soul that she'll bloom.
I plant my heart amongst roses.
So she learns that you must be open.
If you plan to evolve.

Scent

When I was yours,
The scent of loneliness,
Latched itself onto me.
When I freed myself,
The scent of contentment,
Followed my every move.
I was lonely in your arms.
I'm alone now.
And it doesn't feel like it.

Champion

You were once etched into my heart.
I've healed with so much finesse.
Just when I thought you were winning.
I regained control of the game.
I made my move as a queen should,
And came out the champion.

Denial

Deep denial is normal.
The overwhelming feeling of,
"This can't be."
But *it can be, and it is.*
You will move on.
You must free yourself,
From the master lock of denial.
Grab your key of acceptance,
And run towards happiness.

Butterflies

I'm still afraid of the light flutters,
The dancing hues of spring renewal,
The swarming feeling of butterflies.

Lesson

There would be no lesson learned.
If I never lost myself in you.
I learned to appreciate small things.
Like genuinely being listened to,
And feeling admired by my lover.
I am not obligated to deal with infidelity.
I am worth more than inconsistency.
I don't have to tolerate mistreatment.
I deserve a love that shakes my soul.

Baggage

I won't have a rebound.
That would be cruel of me.
I am hauling tons of baggage.
How can I throw this weight?
Onto the balanced shoulders,
Of an innocent soul.
They didn't sign up for this.
Us and our baggage claim games.
I'm shedding the suitcases of us.
They'll be at lane seven,
Waiting for you to claim them,
As rightfully yours.

Self-care

A rose petal bath,
Daisy-scented lotion,
Bittersweet coffee,
My notebook and pen,
It's a self-care day.

Regret Will Bloom

Your mind will never be free of me.
In the quietest moments,
You'll remember my loud laugh.
In your loneliest moments,
You'll remember my warm touch.
In your darkest moments,
You'll remember my glowing light.
The way I recklessly lit up your life.
Brighter than billboards in the city.
You'll remember your betrayal,
And regret will bloom in your heart.

Identify

Identify what is blocking your growth.
Only then will you start to heal.
Wounds must be treated precisely.

Soothe

I cried flowing streams of blue skies.
As the sun patiently waited to rise.
To soothe me and wipe my eyes.
Before the clouds tripled in size.

Materials

I'm stronger than ever before.
You think you built me.
But I carried each brick myself.
As I put myself back together.
I picked the best materials.
So no one like you,
Will ever enter here again.

Old Friend

You feel like an old friend now.
Like my very first best friend.
She moved away without notice.
But each day, I still missed her.
Then time transformed and passed.
She became nothing but a memory.
The friend that *got away,* and now,
It's you, and I hold on to that.
Just as my heart healed before,
It will again.
I will be okay.

Joys

I bathe in small joys.
I give the most meaning,
To the tiniest things.
This way I'm grateful,
For everything.

Live

It's time to start living.
I will live for sunsets,
Cloudy days,
White roses,
Fresh coffee,
Good poetry,
Great music,
I will live for everything.

You Are the Guy

Why do I continue to write about you?
Maybe you're the perfect heartbreak.
The one I consistently run back to.
You think it's a compliment.
The way I twirl my pen to write about you.
You should be offended, ashamed even.
Your wicked soul caused this much pain.
How does it feel to be a symbol?
Not only to me but to the girls who read it.
You are the guy who broke their heart too.
See, I write about you, about our end,
But I also write about their heartbreaker.
You are the guy absorbing thousands of hearts.
So don't feel honored, *we don't honor you.*
We honor the end of us; we honor the end of them.
And I give them hope, that they can heal too.

Spark

I just got my spark back.
The glittering sensation,
That floats within my eyes.
So, I can't love you, I'm sorry.
I was blind for far too long,
It's time to love me now.

Veil

When the veil lifted from my eyes,
I let go of the broken thinking.
The wicked pattern of negativity.
That I blindly fell into.

Maybe It's Magic

I may be caged, but I am not caught.
I'll believe in magic, fairies, and genies.
If the sky came falling from my mouth,
On the day in which you could tame me.
I'm a Widow spider too massive for you.
How could *you, a moth,* defeat me?
I live in royalty, and I breathe the throne.
How could *you, a peasant,* seize it?
I'm a lioness always hunting for prey.
How could *you, a lizard,* survive?
I may be caged within the maze of me.
But caught by you, that I'll never be.

Compatible

I thought we were compatible.
But sun nor moon signs,
Sprinkle watercolor patterns.
You painted your true colors,
As I laid myself on the canvas.
I was completely covered.
In a thousand different hues.
The moment I realized,
I was never a suitable lover.
For the insatiable paintbrush,
Controlled by your hands.

<u>Positivity</u>

I talk to myself,
Not in a peculiar way.
Like a close friend,
Or someone I love.
I assure my heart,
With the same kindness,
That I give to others.
Feed yourself positivity.

Programmed

I gave myself,
Mind, body, and soul.
To someone unworthy.
They wanted to reshape me.
Into some warped version,
Of whom they wanted me to be.
With one goal in their mind.
To strip me of all my power.
My resistance to their lies.
But I cannot be programmed.
Nor can my heart be hypnotized.
I saw through their lies.
Here in this body,
My power comes alive.

Renovations

I am closed for renovations.
Don't call, I won't answer.
Don't knock, I won't hear it.
Don't disrupt my healing.
I'll be open for business soon.
With new stairs to my soul,
Fresh paint on my heart's walls,
And new rules signed by my mind.

Catastrophe

I thought you were the catastrophe.
The one I have feared my whole life.
But now I know you were never that.
You were a tiny hiccup in my life.
You are the gum I accidentally stepped on.
You are the bus I missed by a few seconds.
You do not hold the power to be a catastrophe.
You are a minor and temporary annoyance.
You can't destruct this soul full of peace.

The Lights

The lights dance in hypnosis,
They twist me into their trance.
I can't shift my body an inch.
Unless it's following their sway.
The moonlit midnight blue sky,
Ignites my withering heart,
As it sets my old ways ablaze.
I am alive, this is being alive.
I am more profound than the ocean.
I am the powerful force that crashes.
Like colliding plunging waves.
I devour the shore and trees.
I am free from the gloomy valleys.
I am ready for sunnier strolls.
Along the west coast beaches.
I'm indebted for this gift, this change,
That the light has bestowed upon me.

Affirm:

The trauma you left me is real.
But I am not those traumas.
I am setting the traumas free.

Oh My, New Life

Behind my broken heart,
There was a door to fulfillment.
So, the tragedy was worth it.
Without the final breaking,
There would be no entering.
And oh my,
How could I miss this *new life?*

I love you. I will always love you. I loved you. I no longer love you. Maybe I still love you; All of these are fine. Heartbreak is slow and healing is slower. **Embrace the confusion.** You will see the light soon.

Remember, **heartbreak is temporary.**
This poem is for the *survivors.*

Survivor

You are a survivor.
After winning a war you thought you'd lose.
Fighting to survive while being destroyed.
Making a way to get through all the chaos.

You are a survivor.
By diving headfirst into this battle,
With no protective steel armor and shields.
As you are powerful exposed and bare.

You are a survivor.
As you heal your wounds after the storm.
By the grace of your sun-dusted touch,
The resilience that thrives within your mind,
And an ability to ride the mightiest waves.

Write a letter to your heartbreaker:

Write a letter of empowerment to yourself or who you used to be. If not a letter, write some affirmations or *both:*

"The most exciting, challenging, and significant relationship of all is the one you have with yourself. And if you find someone to love the you, you love, well, that's just fabulous."

-Carrie Bradshaw, *Sex and the city.*

About the Author

Hope is an author and student based in the US. She is pursuing a degree in English Writing and plans to attend film school after graduation. Since she was young, Hope has had a story to tell and a vivid imagination.

As of 2022, she has published five poetry collections, "Tidal Waves of Love," "Infinity," "Breaking Waves," “111 Wings” and "Green Trees and Things." Hope's work touches on love in all facets, healing, empowerment, grief, and so much more.

Hope finds joy in creating art and learning new things. She's at peace when helping animals, drinking coffee, analyzing films, being surrounded by loved ones, or taking a walk-through New York City.

Additionally, Hope has been working on her first romance novel and screenplay. In the future, she hopes to become a noted author, screenwriter, and filmmaker.

Connect with Hope on these social media channels:

Instagram: @byhopemoore

Tik Tok: @byhopemoore

Twitter: @byhopemoore

Tumblr: @byhopemoore

Facebook: Hope Moore

Pinterest: @byhopemoore

You can purchase signed copies of Hope's books, framed poems, poem mugs, and more merchandise on her website! (Byhopemoore.com)

Printed in Great Britain
by Amazon